ASSAULT on NATURE

POETRY BY

GARY BECK

Winter Goose Publishing

Winter Goose Publishing
2701 Del Paso Road, 130-92
Sacramento, CA 95835

www.wintergoosepublishing.com
Contact Information: info@wintergoosepublishing.com

Assault on Nature

COPYRIGHT © 2013 by Gary Beck

First Edition, December 2013

Paperback ISBN: 978-1-941058-00-8

Cover Art by Winter Goose Publishing
Typeset by Odyssey Books

Published in the United States of America

To Robert
who finds this life as strange, yet as familiar, as I do
and perseveres

Poems from *Assault on Nature* have appeared in: The Hiss Quarterly, Nuvein Magazine, Clark Street Review, HazMat Review, Kritya Poetry Journal, Thorny Locust, Death Metal Poetry, Strange Road, decomP, The Blue House, Miller's Pond, High Altitude Poetry, MadSwirl, Bolts of Silk, New Verse News, Poetic Curfews, Enigma, Farmhouse Journal, Words Words Words, Apt Magazine, Blue Fog Journal, Juice Magazine, Sea Stories, Inscribed, Flash Fire, The Delinquent, Robot Melon, Halfway Down the Stairs, Emuse, Polse Guera, Gloom Cupboard, Poems Niederngasse, Foame, Poetic Curfews, The Vertin Press, The Angry Poet, The Cat's Meow, Thirteen Myna Birds, Blinking Cursor Literary Magazine, The Golden Lantern, Callused Hands, The Other Herald, Shine Magazine, Eviscerator Heaven, Asphodel Madness, Adagio Verse Quarterly.

Contents

Media

Powerful light splits the night.
Cameras and crew lust the suffering
that is the entertainment of the people.
Trapped in violet despair,
the helpless victims can't escape
the consuming dance of TV.

Urban Collapse

Decay past
is easier to forget
when it no longer affects us.
The signs of ruin
do not cause us pain,
distanced by time.

Decay present
is easy to ignore,
for we prefer not to see it.
The spread of slums
numbs our frail cities,
consuming us with profits.

Decay future
is easiest to reject,
or else we must prevent it.
The violence to come
is too unpleasant to believe,
which dooms us to destruction.

Further Evolution

Death was once given to us
courtesy of Mother Nature
and there was a basic order,
not fully appreciated
by reluctant participants,
but finally accepted
with a minimum of fuss.
Then man began to interfere
with the evolutionary scheme,
the reliable tried and true
predictable techniques
famine, hunters, accident, old age,
the primary organized mayhems
that served us well a long, long time.
So removal of the unwanted
suddenly started to receive
supplemental assistance.
Murder, manslaughter, massacres,
arson, explosion, electrocution,
hanging, shooting, stabbing,
the endless fatal innovations
by the most destructive life form
on this planetary body
(and possibly any other),
may sweep the solar system,
galaxy, universe,
quite free of any indigenous
less ruthless, less ferocious
alien adversary
awaiting our gift
of thorough destruction.

Tyranny

When our lords and masters
lived high on the hill
they were easily identified
perched behind secure walls,
stouter than peasant thatch
so readily blown down
by ravaging marauders.

We raised our glances up
with envy and desire,
yet we knew our place
was never in the castle.
If we disturbed those above
they invited us to leave town
and we were lucky to escape.

We could hate our oppressors
while we toiled in our place,
but at least we always knew
we were owned by another.
Life was clear, if not simple,
unlike today, when consumers
never know their ruler's face.

Strife

In the eternal struggle
between the nobles
and the people,
the ranks of the forgotten
are filled by new recruits
who meet their untimely end,
victims of those who eat cake,
yet begrudge a crust of bread
to those who toil for them.

City of Struggle

My blood has not penetrated
your concrete face.
My fears have not found comfort
from your metal scowl.
The bold assaults I launched
upon your arrogant towers
failed to win your treasures,
leaving me without tomorrows,
denied the dream of yesterdays.

Cash or Charge

Bayonets are seldom put on broomsticks
by housewives struggling to reach the counters
of overloaded supermarkets, crammed with
frozen, pre-cooked, dehydrated abundance
newest and bestest guaranteed
to feed your family
while the rest of the world
goes hungry.

Unsung Heroes

We owe our thanks to the missile men
who lurked in the underground holes
month after month, year after year,
obedient to the chain of command
and never pushed the buttons
that always beckoned temptation
to transform Terra to Luna.

So sing a song of praise
to the missile men
who resisted temptation . . .

Have you seen the missile men,
the missile men, the missile men?
Have you seen the missile men,
rusting in their silos?

Isolation

In combustible chambers
aloneness gathers
sparking an ecstasy of panic
white heat fast
tremoring
details of confinement
furthering exile,
allowing no appeal.

Sea Change

Mermaids no longer aid
the shipwrecked mariner
and prevent betrayals
by safely observing from afar
the feast of the ravenous shark.

For Tomorrow

We sing not greetings from charred lips
passioning mad lies and cruel inventions,
innocence foregone, though hungered for.
These tall hopes, swirled on uncalm waters.

Journeys sweet additions to the soul
buoyed by a multiplicity of strangers
each a sum doomed to calculations
made in swift reckonings, our aloneness.

How strange the newness of an unknown land
the greener grass of imaginings
losing not self, nor scorning roots
birthing new seed in transportations.

War on Nature

Intelligence appointed us
defenders of mother nature.
Greed invented new ways
to abuse our trusteeship.

War Song

His name is McNamara
he's the leader of the band
of venal politicians
who think that war is grand.

Oh the bullets fly, our leaders lie,
our conscience goes to sleep.
We watch the war on TV sets
and we forget to weep.

So the next time the war bells chime
to invade another land,
remember McNamara
might cause Custer's last stand.

Ghost Ships

Long departed vessels
melted down for scrap,
now razors, TVs, autos,
made from relics of the sea
to profit us once again.

Disintegrated piers
splintering to fragments,
gnawed upon by avid worms,
deserted by travelers
when they found new transport,
now skating rinks and homeless havens.

Cruise ships still sail everywhere
for recreational pursuits,
assaulting unspoiled coasts,
but seldom in conflict
with the perils of the deep,
lest the crew, like rats,
abandon ship.

System

A meritocracy may be
the surest possibility
to continue democracy,
since profit should not be the measure
of access to the public treasure.

'Tis the Season

Now the Christmas cries are silent,
the New Year jubilation's past
and our revels have subsided,
the celebration did not last.

Accelerated greed relaxes
acquisition and envy fade
purchases and payments falter,
time for reckonings to be made.

There is only hope to be
repentant for our season's sin.
When the world ends for you and me
indulgent moneychangers win.

Gravity

Gravity's got me down,
got me tight in its grip.
Don't matter how I try,
I can't shake loose of it.

I'd like to fly up, away
and catapult far beyond
the malicious clutch of earth,
but gravity grinds me down,
pulls me to the final crash.

To B.B.

Your roots did not sink deep enough
into the prejudice of the earth to cling,
when strong winds blew too frequently.

You could not control tomorrow,
yet despite the pliant perils
abided briefly, but with grace.

Nomads

Listen neighbors,
distance and the humming,
a ghostly caravan,
silks, spices, jewels,
women full of babies,
they come, they come.
Who will greet them?
The vacant street blows dust,
the townsfolk make no welcome,
not me, not me,
doors closed to the invader.
They pass windows of rejection.
They cry loneliness of the road.
The men stand stiff with journeys,
full of yearning and shame.
Sorrow, moans the wind,
the unwelcome are departed.

Golden Horde I

She is not coming,
no
and will never come again.
I will pass the many midnights
helpless
like an amputee.
I shall not find
forgetfulness,
rehabilitation,
or opiate stupefaction.
I shall continue
haphazard
as a crusade
and let the dark Saracen
slash my armor,
as
I pass
the weary dimness
in pusillanimous
imaginings.

Golden Horde II

You occupied me
like a Tartar,
raping,
looting,
pillaging.
And I
suffering
like a captive city
hoping
to survive the endless violations,
bent my will,
my knee.
Now immune to trampling
I watch your bannered host
disappear
into the voracious maw
of prosperity.

Bridge

Impassable gaps and rivers once stopped man,
until tired of being eaten, drowned, trapped,
found a log placed well enough for passage,
daringly crossed over and safely entered
the promised land of engineering.

Ode to Dave Dawson and Freddie Farmer

I remember your books
blighting my childhood lust for learning,
reading you over and over,
when nothing else was left.
You were always winning;
sometimes wounded, but always winning.
Vacuum sealed for freshness, inventive,
heroic, resourceful, and always winning.
The Japs, the Jerries, so easily defeated,
you would have even beaten the commies,
but I grew up, ending your wars.
Today a man,
I smile your asinine morality
that rooted in my child's mind
and wonder what you did for fun
after crushing the enemy.

Ruminations

We've poured enough concrete
on our tattered land
to silence the crying earth.

We honor the wine steward
and despise the farmer.

If moonlight washed away our sins,
would we dance the night of hope?

The massacres of people
are better, worse, the same,
as daily butcheries
of fish, fowl, lion, lamb.

We've covered the earth with cities,
as aimless as the urgent ants.

I'm glad Thanksgiving comes but once a year,
the victims wouldn't survive another meal.

Rope

And on some unknown day
man created rope
and it was good to pull.
Rope immediately established
more order in the unstable world,
as long as someone held one end.

And has pulled mankind to power,
necks, mules, carts, ships, planes
brought the goods, tolled the bells,
hanged the innocent and the guilty.
Knots, snares, lassos, ladders
have saved us from disaster,
weaving countless ties.

Little Dreams

Count the number of just so little dreams
and if you have ten fingers enough,
slowly darling you almost missed one,
you will barely find ten shy friends
when pressed will visit an impatient moment
not so long to make you feel most sure,
'cause just so little dreams
smile stiff-jawed too.

Into the Valley

Our troops will trudge from Germany
to the consuming pyres of Bosnia,
to join another ancient war
that's only waiting to resume
the feast on flesh of innocence.

There nestless birds have lost their songs.

Hatred dances on the grim parapets
of furious fortresses of vengeance,
where our young men will be sacrificed
on altars of atonement, thirsting their blood.

There limbless children have no playmates.

Moslem, Christian, east, west,
kings and sultans lead their followers
into the chaos of sword, rifle, missile,
blessed instruments of destruction
improved over the ages for pleasure.
Ambushers lurk on the highways,
searching for omens.

Childhood

Across the courtyard
the lurking eyes of night
spy on their neighbors.
The drone of rancid wives,
the howl of sour husbands
drowns out the screams
of neglected children.
The cry, the curse, the brutal hand
are all the children understand.
They already dread tomorrow,
foreseeing their harsh future.

Aspiration

This our land
unfree to some
to others great,
to most a giant of indifference
(we watch our ballgames,
build our homes,
neglect to guide our children,
forget our president's assassination),
should be as we should be,
struggling to betterment
to find the lost truth,
a kinder wisdom,
instead of submerging
into evildoing and uncaring
that will subvert survival.

Detached Mission

I understand why pilots,
flying planes, pregnant,
with a belly full of bombs,
do not care
that they can obliterate
the cities of the world.
For I have looked down
from high above the strangling clouds,
where I could not see
men crawling like vermin
through squalid streets
of polluted cities,
fleeing ravaged houses
that no longer protect children,
and are far below
compassion's visit.

Journey

If you I touch,
not just your body,
although it pleasures me,
but some mysterious part
of kind hands, comfort,
that does not crumble
at my impatient touch,
how far I travel
on your highways
mutilated stranger,
distant as stars.

Return

Hostage tree,
your yellow streamers
flow with liberty.
The calculating city melts
as the heroes return
to pro bono ovation.
The Great White Way welcomes them
and America no longer worries,
lulled by ticker tape flurries.

A Passage to Spring

For man to circumvent darkness
drabbed by short days,
chilled and untwinkling
with sudden spurts of lust
to roll in grass fields
poke-tickilish to clutching bodies
with only dreams of union,
remembered those frigid evenings
of robes and mufflers,
not relics of passion, sniffles only,
reckless groping towards hope of thaw.

Defeat

Weary me
and sullen you,
the night grows old,
the search grows cold
the last heart has but one pulse
and dissension shall be queen.
If I never wake
and remain the dream
and spend our nights in bitter myth,
like strained fingers creeping over Braille,
touch will never end my vision
for the midnight harpist strums,
plucks the dreamless melody
and I sing silent songs,
sincere as flower children's pads,
while the plaster Buddha
squats and broods.

Transient

The old tom cat of scars and stealth
pads starving streets and famished alleys
alert to all the hands that strike,
passing in a mist of precaution.

City fugitive by day
dodging the foot and the curse,
springing boldly into night
seeking battle, food, a mate.

A few brief moments of pleasure,
a daring yowl of delight,
the rigid survival remembrance,
nine lives are never enough.

Casualty

When I shall die
and am no longer there
in the momentary memory
we used to share,
remember me not
for what caused pain.

I left humanity,
abandoned friends, family,
strangers, and enemies.
Why shouldn't they spurn
my need to return.

Pain was my father
it nurtured me,
love became my mother
and set me free.

Catch of the Day

He died in disunity
crying,
we shall never wake again
and never look upon
regiments of lustful eyes
casting like fishermen,
urgent to take you home
and cook you for their mothers.

Winter Vision

Park Avenue icy street
an old woman slips,
slides downtown
enveloping the city
in winter-veined thighs.
The last policeman
blows his whistle,
dreaming of issuing a summons
for reckless suction.

Opera

The glitter of evening
was there, was there,
the black ties
the coiffured hair,
the designers smiles
and patronizing voices
that rose from the pit
to the astronomer's perch
atop the last balcony.
The women were gowned,
the men were renowned,
the music and settings were grand,
only . . .
The singing was drab.

Tick, Tock

Before we began to tell time
toilers urgently made haste,
while the unambitious lingered.
The daily course of life
was ordered, simple, clear;
sleep, rise, eat, fear,
regulated by guess or gods.
Sundial, hourglass, windup,
the hands began to turn
and mankind turned faster,
rushing to overtake
life's departing moments.

Pollution

The baggage of waste
bends the bloody head
of weary mother nature,
as she slowly surrenders
to the mindless assault
of her greedy children,
who can only hope and dream
that dawn will come again
and heal earth's tainted crust.

Habitat

The order of things
natural and contrived
is dissolving.
Our laws serve injustice.
Our streets are congested
with the ill, the lost, and the mad.
Our hopes are upscale fashions.
Our dreams are sleek electronics.

We have forgotten
the tremble fear of thunder,
open fields of disobedient flowers,
rain pattering on leafy shelter.
Generations of cities
have stunted
the order of things.

Calculation

Do not dare remain a child
unless insured from poverty,
for wealth buys opportunity.

In the cash drawer of the soul
frequent users trade away
the right to dream another day.

Whatever claims we hope to stake
in gold mines of prosperity
are lost in kind adversity.

Two Visions

I
Dawn in cities
is the quietest time,
before the daily sacrifices
of our citizens.

II
Money buys immunity
from responsibility
with comforting ingenuity.

Denial

I joined you
a moment of hunger
unsated, birthed
deception, crushing
seeds of love's
conceptions.

I was unworthy, beloved.

Unwilling to allay
feelings of revulsion
that followed betrayal
measured by others,
esteem lost
in greedy pleasure.

I was callous from hunger.

I left you
aware that our climax bed
could not long be shared,
ended our fierce union
which languished somewhere
beyond endurance.
I murdered delight.

Deliverance

Puny dreamer of caravans
riding the subway
freighted
with mindless drools
dead, but seemingly sleeping,
rattle the paper every corpse
for stations
(time for motions of illusion)
come like ermine visions,
conductors soliloquy mumbled,
then
the Canal Street of the soul.

Condition Dangerous

Government by fools
is what we deserve
when we neglect vital issues.
Participation in representative government
is not a convenience, but an exertion.
The marriage of television and politics
starts the honeymoon with the devil.
It may not be too late to discover
the only thing worse than our candidates
are our elected officials,
giving us 2001 problems
and only 1979 solutions.

Transaction

Night city of a million fingers of ambition,
beckoning to strangers from mysterious windows
concealing the sons and daughters of privilege,
surrendering themselves for survival.

Before the warmth of morning grins
a welcome to the fleeing stars
the city trembles from delicious dew,
devouring the offspring of the advantaged.

Neglect

We listened to the good advice
of elders, uncles, counselors,
got an education,
got a good career,
made money,
made more money,
profited from our times.

We never listened attentively,
concealing our boredom
behind the mask of interest,
but we recollected enough advice
so at decision making time
we should have been equipped
to grapple with the crucial issues
that concerned earth, air, water.

Instead we elected or appointed
the unready, ill-prepared, unfit,
to regulate the way of life.
And they socially presided as our future
was pillaged, polluted, poisoned,
until blighted landscapes, seascapes, airscapes
became our prized inheritance.

Vision of Tomorrow

After I am gone
the world may regain its senses,
conclude the war with nature
and build a new tomorrow
of peaceful coexistence,
for which I would sacrifice
although I wasn't entirely responsible
for terrible conditions.

Prevent Cruelty

Their name sounds reassuring,
which must please public and private
persons, who accept their basic business,
the mass destruction of the unwanted
cats, dogs, and other inconvenient life.

Should we give responsibility
for elimination of the unfit,
useless rejects, discards, biters
to the mercy of humane societies?

Sneak Attack

The greatest form of slavery
is mindless watching of TV.

Decay

Decay
will never be arrested
in a single day,
or in our fragile future,
crumbling the strength of cities,
polluting the fields and forests,
as we lose the final hope
of escape
from a doomed planet.

Future Hope

Someday of visions
we shall see
wondrous towers
of marvelous construction
rising from the rubble
of neglected cities,
sheltering our people
from casual destruction.

Felon

Child of few summers
you are born to poverty
and will never know serenity,
once begotten by man.

Somehow your genes spilled
into a teen mother
who could not find another
nurturer of sons.

School feared and hated you
and prepared you with derision,
for crimes, drugs, the streets, prison,
victim of indifference.

Hit Song

This is the computer age,
so don't waste time talking beauty.
Carbon monoxide gets its song.
Strontium 90 gets its song.
Even irradiated ergosterol has a song.
So don't waste precious time
writing about trees or birds,
praise air pollution.

Urban Vision

The clerks at lunchtime
are almost a song,
walk backwards if you have no eyes.
They hunger for visions,
but only find distorted lust.
The last hand offers no assistance.
Old cigar butts sprout on streets
like bamboo jungles,
revealing liberal predators.
The young girls pass,
ball bearings in their buttocks,
greased by fezzed old men,
searching for conventions.

Raise the Speed Limit

It is inky night.
We are driving, driving, driving
into the impenetrable bleakness
of coronary America.
There are no stars left,
just never-ending darkness,
broken only by flashing lights
from wanderers forever lost
in high speed car crashes.

Pre-Dawn

The city sits
a patient vulture
in a predatory trance,
waiting to stir and devour
restless youth of no hopes,
shattered by neglect,
nurtured on abuse,
battered by despair,
in a world that does not care.
The city wakes
and hones its beak
and listens to the rumble
of its empty belly.

Seasonal Change

Well,
gee whiz,
astronomers is really right.
It's still cold,
the frigid wind blows like mad,
the skirts are trying to expose thighs
and all this time
I'm sitting at my desk,
surrounded by slaves of profit,
who can't hear me singing,
spring . . .
Spring . . .

Union

However
reflections come, go,
remain sullenly poised,
posing in some venereal show,
passing in venal promenade,
wines on an east river terrace.
The blonde cannibal smiles,
her ravenous mouth
corrupt with midnight couplings,
that beautiful mouth
how many nights fastened on mine,
then gushing obscenities,
until our bodies joined
like two ferocious beasts,
finally screaming comecomecomemmme,
afterwards falling apart,
two strangers in a soiled bed,
strangers with dirty souls.

Rebirth

The last sleep
of armless brothers
allows a dream.
Sing the serpent,
ride the waterfall of time,
wake the forgotten poet,
grow new arms from royal palms,
careless as some god of myth,
strewing seed to restless winds.

Incompletions

Endeavors in the world expand
the struggle for continuance,
a crazed collector, amassing art
not quite oxygen enough to go around
and competitive respiration harms
man, beast, insect, plant,
all staggering separately,
under the most determined assault
that man the marauder has ever mounted
against mother nature.
And if ears grow dull from incessant throb
of machine, siren, explosion, shriek, sob;
the child laugh, bird trill, man music
will pierce the encrustation
of a thousand deafening screams
relieving the pillars of the skull,
however briefly, of their burden;
eyes, greatest gift after brain,
design attributed to unknown master
may let us see another moment
with our limited video vision,
of wondrous nature.

Union II

Yes, heart,
again hiding in sabotage
without her.
Walking aimlessly on explosive streets,
a couple passes me.
He curses her:
"Keep your lousy clothes
and television set. I wish
I never met you."
I feel the same tonight.
I cannot tell her though.
She lies with someone else.

I gape inside
as mucousy as new-hatched life.
No one licks the after-birth away.
Yes, heart, wait.
Tomorrow night we'll lie together,
her head cradled in my neck,
hand upon my belly,
but then the next night and the next.
My love gives birth to pain.

Our embrace is mellowed by hatred.
We hack like ancient axmen
until our bird collapses, then we pause,
naked in our fear
and resurrect with patches
our battered remains.

Buccaneer

Cartagena, you have betrayed me
and would again,
if I escape the hangman.
Your past promises were taken
for delights too soon forgotten,
spent as fast as wasted treasure
concealed ancient pools of blood,
spilled with pleasure.

Columbine

Wild flower, Columbine,
brief bloom of alpine clime,
a treasured concubine
of some now departed time.

Accounting

In the soul's per annum bank
clerks in tiny cages, bored,
trapped like misers, rank on rank,
count the treasure that they hoard.
The increase we hope to earn,
portion of our daily needs,
sought in promise of return
for the efforts of our deeds.

Prey

Birds of unsoft eyes
flown by women with thin beaks
and sharp tongues,
swoop down upon our weakness,
as silent as surgeons
entering flesh.

Anguished Vision

I will not be a fading man
of tired words, yearning lost places.
I've cultivated city streets
and paved the desolate forests,
the passing visions of strangers,
the wandering cries that deny rest,
sing sleepless nights of twisted hopes,
that plague will spare our greedy land,
as it's carried by fur creatures
rushing to be coats for seniors,
their shabby banner of protest
the sad flush of expectations,
passing the days like wringing hands
fluting each other in despair,
blind to the moment of conquest
that squanders dawn's deliverance.

Disadvantaged

Only a temple priest
high above the street swirl,
doesn't go down from dreams
into the harsh world.

Endurance

Endurance is the lot of man
if we would survive the test of time,
wars, plague, famine, progress,
the decay of crumbling empires,
the discovery of new frontiers,
where the voices of hatred are silent,
the cries of despair are forgotten,
the smiles of destruction are departed,
the liberal grasp, the urgent greed,
are mostly extinguished.

Unto Day

Struggles are slower
than conflagrations
and often require
bicker and barter
to avert threats,
alienation.
Nothing is resolved
in one decisive stroke,
thrust to conclusion,
totalitarian end,
grasping isolation
the sum of enterprise,
under or over achievements.

Urbana

Glittering lights
speak cities to strangers,
kissing the congested distance,
the promenade through sensual streets,
the bus rides through sleaze town,
the unknown route to exile,
the rapid transit to discovery.

Crash Landing

After moon set
wing tips lost in darkness
flickering lights at 30,000 feet
transit the airborne traveler.
Centuries below
clouds pitter patter
little girl toes
digging in the sand.
The endangered bird
flails the air,
hiccups an octopus explosion
that frees the stewardess,
rigid smile waxed in place,
offers coffee, tea, chocolate,
as the last hand gropes blindly,
veins surfacing in the pantry,
reaching for survival.

Continued War on Nature

The illuminations of the world
are fibrous curtains,
constructions of confusion,
the fear of nuclear eruptions,
economic deprivations
social rejections,
last remnants poisoned
by ominous mushroom clouds.
As the world shifts to sand
the dream for green tomorrows
leaves only a backward glance,
a yearning for illusion.

About the Author

Gary Beck has spent most of his adult life as a theater director. He has had numerous published works including *Dawn in Cities* (Winter Goose Publishing), *Days of Destruction, Expectations,* and his novel, *Extreme Change,* published by Cogwheel Press. Gary has also had several original plays and translations produced off Broadway, in New York City where he currently resides.

Follow Gary on his website: ***garycbeck.com***

www.ingramcontent.com/pod-product-compliance
Lightning Source LLC
Chambersburg PA
CBHW071505070426
42452CB00041B/2298